By & By

Poems by Don Gutteridge and John B. Lee

By & By

Poems by
Don Gutteridge
and
John B. Lee

First Edition

Hidden Brook Press
www.HiddenBrookPress.com
writers@HiddenBrookPress.com

Copyright © 2020 Hidden Brook Press
Copyright © 2020 Don Gutteridge and John B. Lee

All rights for poems revert to the author. All rights for book, layout and design remain with Hidden Brook Press. No part of this book may be reproduced except by a reviewer who may quote brief passages in a review. The use of any part of this publication reproduced, transmitted in any form or by any means, electronic, mechanical, photocopied, recorded or otherwise stored in a retrieval system without prior written consent of the publisher is an infringement of the copyright law.

Title: By & By
Authors: Don Gutteridge and John B. Lee

Cover Image: Richard M. Grove
Cover Design: Richard M. Grove
Layout and Design: Richard M. Grove

Typeset in Garamond
Printed and bound in Canada
Distributed in USA by Ingram,
       in Canada by Hidden Brook Distribution

Library and Archives Canada Cataloguing in Publication

Title: By & by / poems by Don Gutteridge and John B. Lee.
Other titles: By & by (2020) | By and by
Names: Gutteridge, Don, 1937- Miniature musings.
      Lee, John B., 1951- Small pleasures.
Description: Poems.
Identifiers: Canadiana (print) 20200329588
        Canadiana (ebook) 20200329677
        ISBN 9781989786109 (softcover)
        ISBN 9781989786116 (ebook)
Subjects: LCSH: Canadian poetry—21st century.
      CSH: Canadian poetry (English)—21st century.
Classification: LCC PS8293.1 .B9 2020
        DDC C811/.5408—dc23

Table of Contents

And Furthermore: a preface to By & By – *p. 2*

Miniature Musings
By Don Gutteridge

– Touch – *p. 6*
– Amber – *p. 7*
– Linked – *p. 8*
– Moniker – *p. 9*
– Romance – *p. 10*
– Bloodless – *p. 11*
– Vet – *p. 12*
– Gait – *p. 13*
– Pluck – *p. 14*
– Breech – *p. 15*
– Praise – *p. 16*
– Throb – *p. 17*
– Greening – *p. 18*
– Gibbous – *p. 19*
– Boredom – *p. 20*
– Moot – *p. 21*
– Regret – *p. 22*
– Summer in the Time of Plague – *p. 23*
– In the Bone – *p. 24*
– Hallelujah – *p. 25*
– Wedding Day: 1915 – *p. 26*
– Serene – *p. 27*
– Caruso – *p. 28*
– Stories – *p. 29*
– Bauble – *p. 30*
– Conversation – *p. 31*
– Ambush – *p. 32*
– Craft – *p. 33*
– Naivite – *p. 34*

– Blizzard – *p. 35*
– Poor – *p. 36*
– Cocoon – *p. 37*
– Fit – *p. 38*
– Matinee – *p. 39*
– Match – *p. 40*
– Hope – *p. 41*
– Utterly – *p. 42*
– One Summer – *p. 43*
– Tailgunner – *p. 44*
– Awakening – *p. 45*
– Everything Born – *p. 46*
– Minstrelsy – *p. 47*
– Versifier – *p. 48*
– Pied – *p. 49*
– Dream – *p. 50*
– Chrysalid – *p. 51*
– Bloom – *p. 52*
– Stalwart – *p. 53*
– Allure – *p. 54*
– Tactile – *p. 55*
– Time's Tick – *p. 56*
– Moonless – *p. 57*
– Horizon – *p. 58*
– Quip – *p. 59*
– Gist – *p. 60*
– Unbidden – *p. 61*
– Mettle – *p. 62*
– Ajar – *p. 63*
– Galahad – *p. 64*
– Romance – *p. 65*
– Lots – *p. 66*
– Forge – *p. 67*
– Elixir – *p. 68*

– Abed – *p. 69*
– Unalloyed – *p. 70*
– Night Terrors – *p. 71*
– Antedeluvian – *p. 72*
– Dance – *p. 73*
– Tinged – *p. 74*
– Hill – *p. 75*
– Plot – *p. 76*
– Meandering – *p. 77*
– Barelegged – *p. 78*
– Rupture – *p. 79*
– Heaven – *p. 80*
– Breakers – *p. 81*
– Puzzled – *p. 82*
– Promethean – *p. 83*
– Singing – *p. 84*
– Shy – *p. 85*
– Communion – *p. 86*
– Wonder – *p. 87*
– Basso – *p. 88*
– Salute – *p. 89*
– Bone – *p. 90*
– Womb – *p. 91*
– Demesnes – *p. 92*
– Inside – *p. 93*
– Romance – *p. 94*
– Precambrian: Cyprus Lake – *p. 95*
– Time's Tick – *p. 96*
– Oval – *p. 97*
– Chum – *p. 98*
– Legacy – *p. 99*
– Wish – *p. 100*
– Adroit – *p. 101*

Small Pleasures
By John B. Lee

— In the Smallest Disturbance of Earth — *p. 104*
— Chorus Frogs Singing of Spring — *p. 106*
— It Wasn't Always This Way — *p. 107*
— Wonder-filled — *p. 109*
— Morning Song — *p. 111*
— if I am not here, then why ... — *p. 112*
— For All His Dark Dreaming — *p. 114*
— The Bee in the Blossoming Crab — *p. 116*
— Ode to an Oriole Feeding
    Upon an Orange Outside my Window — *p. 185*
— Ideas of Ideal Beauty — *p. 120*
— This Then — *p. 123*
— It Might Have Been Beautiful — *p. 125*
— As Was His Nature — *p. 127*
— Something Dead in the Sun — *p. 129*
— The First Great Dying — *p. 131*
— A Ghost in the Spirit of Stone — *p. 133*
— in light, the colour of creatures — *p. 135*
— ... see how dying draws a crowd — *p. 138*
— The Wild and Lovely World — *p. 140*
— Living Upside Down — *p. 142*
— Sweet Remembering — *p. 144*
— Merry Christmas — *p. 146*
— Mostly the Snow — *p. 148*
— Admonition Against Injury — *p. 150*
— Islands Away from My Hand — *p. 151*
— On Viewing the Super Blood Wolf Moon I
    Contemplate the most frequently asked Google
        Lunar Question: Is the moon real? — *p. 152*
— Parable of the Mouse and the Owl — *p. 153*
— Alive — *p. 155*

– And time – *p. 157*
– And I, This Evident Man – *p. 158*
– At First Light – *p. 160*
– Hawberries on the Silver Lake Trail – *p. 161*
– Still Water, Still Night – *p. 162*
– The Lake in Storm – *p. 164*
– The Vanishing – *p. 165*
– Unseen – *p. 168*
– "… the living things of the world
 are never far from water" – *p. 170*
– A Brief Encounter – *p. 172*
– How Still, how still, how wonderfully still – *p. 173*
– The Day the Potawatomi Woman
 Walked Away and into the Lake – *p. 175*
– The Fox Remains – *p. 177*
– The Step Ladder – *p. 179*
– Young Heroes of Terrace Beach – *p. 180*
– Cycling Home – *p. 182*

Afterword – *p. 185*

Author Bios
 Don Gutteridge – *p. 200*
 John B. Lee – *p. 201*

We shall sing on that beautiful shore
The melodious songs of the blessed;
And our spirits shall sorrow no more,
Not a sigh for the blessing of rest.

lines taken from the lyric "In the Sweet By and By"

And Furthermore: a preface to By & By

I have known Don Gutteridge one way or another since 1970. I first met him as a reader meets a writer. As an eighteen-year old freshman at University of Western Ontario, I found his books in the university bookstore. I was on the hunt for poetry, and UWO bookstore was well stocked in those days with Canadian poets. Gutteridge at first attracted my attention because he was not only local, but he taught as a professor at the very university where I was in attendance. I purchased every book of his that I could find and I was thrilled to discover a wonderful poet.

Four years later I had the privilege of being a student in his English practicum class at Althouse. The reader became the student. Yet, I kept my reading of his work, and my admiration for Don Gutteridge, the writer, a secret.

After spending a decade as a teacher of secondary school English, in 1983/4 I returned to Graduate School at Western. My thesis had the title "Teaching Canadian Poetry in Senior English." My advisor was Governor General Award winning Canadian poet Don McKay. One of the three professors on the acceptance committee was Don Gutteridge.

In the meantime, as a poet in my own rite, I had published my first full-length book in 1976. By the time I was in Graduate school I had published four subsequent titles. I would only remain as a full-time teacher for another five years. In 1989, I defenestrated and I have called myself a full-time author ever since.

In the intervening years I've continued to read every book Don Gutteridge published. I think it would be safe to say that Don considers me to be one of his true readers.

We have become something of a mutual admiration society. We correspond frequently. He sends me his new poems, and I send him mine. We communicate on dozens of topics. We share a belief in the importance of keeping the faith in poetry. Over the past three years I've championed Don Gutteridge by selecting two of his books for inclusion in the *John B. Lee Signature Series* published by Hidden Brook Press. It is under that same imprimatur that we choose to publish *By & By*. The title is nearly eponymous to the hymn that inspired it. The song is something of a spiritual threnody in celebration of the afterlife. I quote the opening verse as an epigram to this collection of poems.

However, despite the reference to the afterlife, I assure you that both Don Gutteridge and I are very much alive, and this won't be the last time you hear from us. I might end this preface with one of my favourite sign offs.

… and furthermore …

John B. Lee
July 12, 2020

Miniature Musings

Don Gutteridge

For Anne in loving memory.

Touch

For Anne in loving memory

We lie in the lee of the dark
and let moonlight flow
molten over us, and thigh
to thigh we tingle with touch,
and I want so much to hold you
till doomsday dawns,
to watch your bedizening eyes
open to me like a slow-
blooming rose, to canonize you
whole and feel you singing
in my soul.

Amber

Tom and I jigging
for pickerel on Cameron's blue
glaze, letting the boat
drift north to south
on the breath of the breeze,
and we ease ourselves into the
amber afternoon until
a big-mouth bass
strikes with a barracuda bite
and we watch it lift with a
whip-lashing whoosh
out of its element like a bent
bow, sashay on its tail,
spit the bait and leave
two fishermen bouche-bé

Linked

For Tom

And once again we find
ourselves on Cameron's lake,
our fishing gear baited
and ready, and an afternoon
slides by as soft as silk
and as rare as a blue moon,
and we dream of the deep dells
below where the big bass
glide, unblinking,
and minnows shiver in the shallows,
and we are comfortable in our own
skin, happy to be here
in one another's company,
sated by sun, linked
by love.

Moniker

For my brother Bob in memoriam

My favourite uncle Christened you
"Googie" from a character in the
funny papers, and "Googie"
you were to all and sundry
in a village numinous with names,
nicknames and monikers
of every ilk, but when you left
the village you left "Googie"
behind, along with the tooth
fairy, Santa and the boogieman,
and after a while it didn't seem
odd to be calling you "Bob."

Romance

Grace Leckie's colt
with a spring in his stutter-step
and a brand-new erection
as ripe as a ruptured rose,
prances in the meadow where the
clover grows, and the girls
look ready to bolt or swallow
their blushes whole, while the boys
wipe the grin from their faces
and wonder aloud how such
a stallion's thing resurrects,
and Coop says, with a wink,
"He's ready for romance!"

Bloodless

Every Saturday afternoon
whatever the season, found us
seated at the aging Imperial,
taking in the double-feature
where the silver screen bristled
with Indians and two-gun
paladins in their sagebrush
sagas, where cutout villains
died bloodlessly for our
amusement and the colour cartoon
catapulted Bugs and Magoo
into our midst before the
cliff-hanging serial
teased and tantalized, and O
how we cheered in renewed
communion when the cavalry arrived
in the nick of time and the disparate
parts of our wondrous world
rhymed.

Vet

For Tom

Even now I see you
moving from farm to farm
and, "doing no harm,"
treating the beasts of the field,
and God's creatures are healed
under your touch as soothing
as the fluting music of Orpheus,
and I remember how
you always loved animals,
how you hugged our malamute
or giggled at a Scottie's impish
antics or calmed our fretting
cat, and you were ever
tugged by love, destined
to metamorphose from boy
to practicing vet.

Gait

We never tired of watching
Shirley and her long-legged
gait over grandfather's
lawn or her drum majorette's
prancing dance with fretted
boots and twirling baton
or the twinkle in her eye, just
for me, that implied, "Here
I am, take the bait!"

Pluck

One lucky day
when June was still jejune,
we gathered in Hendrie's coop
where JoAnne dropped her drawers
without a thought or a blink
to expose the ripe rose
between her thighs,
and the boys, too wise
for their years, on the cusp of lust,
vied to see who was brave enough
to pluck it.

Breech

You welcomed the world feet-
first, as if to say,
"Here I am, I'm me!"
and when I spotted your perfect
brow, unbruised by the lurch
of birth and your eyes greeting
the room blue, my heart
burst like a rapturous rhyme
with a love that would last us
a lifetime.

Praise

The flowers in the Widow Bray's
groomed garden grew
like a soothsayer's predictions:
poppies, gladioli, daisies
in profusions of bloom, licked
biddable by light and nursed
by a tendrill'd touch, and we prayed
that she found some solace
in the praise of a grateful village.

Throb

Cockrobins hob-
nobbing at ease on grandfather's
lawn, dreaming of dew-
worms bloated in the grass,
a song of the season throbbing
in their throat.

Greening

Mrs. Bray's garden was like
that first flowering in Eden
before Eve and the apple,
and though widowed by war,
she moves through the gladioli
and gardenias of her petalled bower
with a Grecian grace, and every
bud she touches bursts
with bloom while the gods
in their greening, smile

Gibbous

It must have been a gibbous
moon that night in Nuremburg
so many years ago
(and too soon gone)
when we lay abed gazing
at the stir of stars tingling
in the unmarred dark
above the breeze-brushed
sill, and we were pleased
just to greet one another
eye to wedded eye
and let ourselves be liberated
by love.

Boredom

Celibate and bored, Eve
dallied among daisies
and daffodils along the groomed
boulevards of Eden, waiting
for a bloom to droop or a bee
to be baffled by honey
or a bullfrog to croon
a Siren song, but nothing
in Paradise grew or seethed
with seed or met a timely
demise, and when an apple
hung succulent on the forbidden
tree, the mother of us all,
unexempt from temptation,
gave it a chew.

Moot

When the great poetaster
fashioned Eden for Adam's
pleasure and, in his haste,
forgot to add passion
to the greenery, so that
when Eve was breathed out of a
spare rib, the mated pair
smiled a lot and admired
the scenery until Eve,
celibate and bored, famished
the forbidden fruit and made
the fate of humankind
moot.

Regret

There wasn't a breath of breeze
in Eden, but then Adam
was no sailor and Eve
no Aphritite,
and it wasn't the sea that un-
did them but rather an appetite
for apples and the ethics of Good
and Evil, and as the ruptured
couple bid adieu
to their paradisal dale,
they paused to think upon
God's oddities and grapple
with the rictus of regret.

Summer in the Time of Plague

I remember well the summer
the pristine beaches of Canatara
were closed, the "No Swimming"
sign propped up in the sand
like a bandaged thumb, and mothers
kept their children handy
in the keep of their kitchen, and we tried
not to notice the friend with a
withered arm or the awkward
angle of a leg-brace,
and nobody knew where or when
"it" would come again
with invisible vibrancy, and we were
afraid to utter that benumbing
phrase: "Infantile paralysis."

In the Bone

I wake from a dream of you
and know you are no longer
with me in the irredeemable
dark of the room we once
loved in, and I feel the moon
looming and the shudder of shadow
across the counterpane,
and I try to bring your face
once again into view,
smiling for me alone,
and I yearn for the soothing bruise
of your embrace to ease the brittle
breaking of my heart and the un-
renounceable ache
buried in the bone.

Hallelujah

When Shirley McCord was still
almost-a-woman, I willed
the bottle to spin her way
and was more than satisfied
at a winning smile, and later
in the day, jumping rope,
she raised her leg so high
I cried Hallelujah
and praised the Lord.

Wedding Day: 1915

Once more I bring this
vintage photo to my adoring
eye: my grandparents
wedding pose with Gramps
in uniform looking every
inch the warrior he was soon
to be, and Gran touching
his sleeve as if she might
loose track of him and smiling
serenely, and I like to think
the love lingering there
between them was enough
to withstand four years
in the grit and grime of Flanders
sanguinary fields, and now
preserved for me in black-
and-white (by a camera
that cannot lie), untinctured
by time.

Serene

Serene in Eden, Adam
soon grew tired
of bluebelles and a dozen
cousins forever in full
bloom, and he longed just
once to pluck a blossom
and watch it shrivel, to feel
something akin
to desire, to be uncivil
to the God who sired him
and rubbed Eve like a genii
out of a random rib to nibble
an apple and leave them both
ungrammared.

Caruso

In Sunday school, Clayton
caroled "Jesus Loves Me"
like a caterwauling Caruso,
and the Reverend Buchanan
rolled his eyes and replied
with a mincing wince, glad
that God was on his side,
and when the plate was passed,
Clayton put his nickel in
and grinned.

Stories

In Sunday school I sang
as if I really believed
that Jesus loved me,
that Adam and Eve grew
wary of their nudity, that Samson
got even with God at Gaza,
that Daniel was delivered, dazzled,
from the lion's den, that Joshua
blew the horn that levelled
the walls of Jericho, that David
felled Goliath with his puncturing
pebble and Ruth stayed
home in Moab, and when
I began to doubt the sparrow's
fall and the stamina of these
stories stuttered, I simply
took their kind of truth
and put it into poems.

Bauble

For Anne in loving memory

You always defended Eve
and her appetite for apples,
(knowing as you did the best
way to resist temptation
is to grapple with it) and you
cheered her on as she bit,
despite the odds that God
would not approve (and Adam,
hobbled by timidity, would nod
and agree): after all,
the agile adder held out
the beguiling Tree like a
a bright bauble – and you,
my love, just smile.

Conversation

For Claire Organ and for Anne in loving memory

Every weekday, prompt
upon the hour, you met
for coffee and girl-talk,
tossing around good-
natured tidbits
of gossip about the foibles
of your fellows (your words unfurling
with the ease of intimacy)
and shared a laugh (or sigh)
at some Trumpian tantrum
or a politician's unfathomable folly
(and occasionally a gentle Jeremiad)
but in truth yours was one
long continental conversation
only Death could silence.

Ambush

In the dappled demesnes of Eden
Adam in his solitude
grew bored with tulips
and hibiscus that never needed
weeding and lambs that frolicked
the afternoons away,
and God in His mercy drew
Eve out of a random rib,
and all was well with the
prenuptial nudes until
Eve ambushed an apple.

Craft

For Judy Hammond Ogletree

One September afternoon
you and I found ourselves
on CCI's debate stage,
and I didn't know you were a
master of the craft and I
was grateful you were on my side
as I tried in vain to untorque
my tongue, while you just
smiled as if disaster
was the furthest thing from your tidy
mind and after all
is said and done, as I remember,
we won.

Naivité

Riding home in the bin
of Bob Leckie's beaten-
down, fender-bent
pick-up, we passed
young Marilyn on her way
to town, and when she waved
we heard Bob whistle
and say, "Now there
goes one sweet
piece!" and Tommy and I
looked at one another
like the gents we were, and wondered
what part of the girl
we admired he meant.

Blizzard

For Anne in loving memory

Outside my window the blizzard
seethes, but here I am warmed
by thoughts of you when you still
breathed for both of us,
of Christmases past with our kids
parsing presents with the
surprise of the season in their eyes
and the gratuitous joy in yours,
and I try my best now
to think of the Babe in His Christian
crib, but I am not yet
reconciled to your leaving, and resentment
hums in my heathen heart

Poor

My dog Moochie was a pleasing
pooch, trailing after me
on our mile-and-a-half trek
to school each day
and mooching bread on the school-
house steps, and when
he was dying of distemper,
my father, unable to afford
a vet, dropped him off
somewhere in the countryside,
where, alone and bewildered,
he might stray into a friendly
farm and find someone
who loved him more than we did,
and I hated my father, not
for abandoning my spaniel,
I hated hm for being poor.

Cocoon

I passed my boyhood days
in a cushioned cocoon, free
of Time's tyranny, and every
morning the world began
anew when the sun rose
over First Bush and set
the streets ablaze (I toddled on)
and sank again into the Baltic
blue of our Lake, while high
above a moon as golden
as a Spaniard's doubloon grazed
the evening sky and shone
down upon our grateful games
and just before sleep seized me
I whispered thanks to the gods
who gave us these gifts
and never asked why.

Fit

I was born with a village in my veins
and weaned on its tempting tillage
and I loved the Dickensian denizens
who peopled my poems and pentameters
for ours was a three-steepled
town where the Bible was ballast
and as real as the sands of Canatara
and I teethed on its teeming stories:
  Sampson dismembering Gaza
  David's deadly pebble
  Zacharias in his trembling tree
  Delilah's treacherous snip
  Moses hushed in the bulrushes
  Sheba's lascivious lip
and all were mine to re-
imagine as I saw fit.

Matiněe

At our Saturday matinée
the hero always wore black
and rode a white horse
(with a nickering neigh) into a
sagebrush saga
and cartoon villains died
bloodlessly for our amusement,
and Cochise, the only good
Indian allowed by the Hollywood
henchmen with a penchant for powwows,
shunned the war-dance
for the pipe of peace, and these
were the stories that fuelled my fancy,
and magnified my imagination,
that I spun into a cornucopia
of plots and poems peppering
the page for seven decades.

Match

My Uncle Tom and I
loved our golf, meandering,
in linked tandem, meadowed
fairways as green as the desmenes
of Eden, and his drives sweetened
the summer's breeze and his wedges
softened the ball aloft
before it settled an inch
from the pin, and I smiled
as he grinned and sunk the putt,
and I think often of those
amiable afternoons, in sunshine
or rain, and that day,
when striving to win a match
that didn't matter, his heart
shattered like a window pane.

Hope

For Anne in loving memory

I miss you most at Christmas
when you were alive in the world
and we thought the leavening love
of our fifty-seven years
would last forever and often
on the Eve of that glorious morning
we would sit on the green chesterfield
and reminisce about gifts
and lean turkey and the wise
eyes of our children jolted
by the joy of sleigh-bells
and antelopian reindeer
in Santa's magical mirage
and we remembered that mangered
Babe in his Christian crib
with the Holy Ghost hovering
above and our hearts unfurled
by hope.

Utterly

Bill Barr's pool
room drew us to its
tantalizing temptations
like moths to a flicker of flame,
but, alas, a discreet curtain
marred out view of the dodgy
doings behind it, and we,
sipping our straw-drawn
Pepsis, were fated to be
mere listeners to the crisp
collision of ball and cue
or the feathered thunk in a far
pocket, and oh how we envied
the denizens inside and longed
for the day we would turn eighteen
and enter that satisfying sanctum
and be corrupted utterly.

One Summer

For Sandra Grocott Gamble

Your hand folded in mine,
we made a bold promenade
along the sidewalks of our home
terrain, all eyes
lingering on your loveliness, and I
was as proud as a peacock
in its plumage, and even though
love bloomed but briefly
for one singular summer,
fading with autumn's languishing
leaves, I remember it still,
almost eighty years on,
feel it still singing
inside.

Tailgunner

Jerry's Dad, the tail-
gunner who survived five
seasons in a glass bubble
with bullets buzzing around him
like berserk bees, couldn't
drink enough booze
to muzzle the maelstrom
of his memories or the furlongs
of regurgitated fears, and his heart
simply hemorrhaged and Jerry
was bereft of the father he idolized,
while mine, who repaired the planes
that limped inland, wizened
in his son's eyes.

Awakening

The sun rises over
First Bush, the lava
of its light like the slow
opening of a June rose,
lacquering the leafage
and rousting robins from their
yellow-beaked sleep,
setting butterflies a-flutter
in the breath of a breeze and then
anointing a village by a Lake
with its lucid layering before
seeping agleam into alleys
and ells, and there on a
sun-strummed street
stands a boy something
like me, navigating the day's
breaking, a-dream with desire,
waiting once again
for the world's awakening

Everything Born

When Eve ambushed the apple,
she swapped Eden for a world
where everything born must die
but not before the first
bloom-burst, before the fecund
fuse of procreation in the Earth's
renewable womb, before the sizzle
of sex and the breech-birth
of poetry to assuage and condole,
and I for one cheered
her cheek, grateful for every
breath I draw that denies
for a day my inexorable end
and leaves me living and wielding
words to celebrate that dappled
garden and Eve's spiteful
bite.

Minstrelsy

In Sunday School we sang
just to hear ourselves sing,
so loud the Reverend Buchanan's
jowls jiggled, our vigorous
vowels ringing the rafters
in jubilant song, all
the while hoping our sins
would be rescinded and that Heaven
would be moved by our minstrelsy.

Versifier

When God blew Adam out of
Eden's dust, He said,
"You must name all the things
I have provided thee,"
and Adam felt his tongue
torque about something
that became a word he heard
himself say "This be a rose,"
and "This a tulip," and Eve,
recently unzipped
from a rib, asked, "What
be these?" and Adam,
searching for the word's
first idea, said "These
be flowers," and, enchanted
by his petal-perfect bower,
added, "You are my red,
red rose, my blood-
blooming tulip," and Eve
knew that Beauty had been
embodied in such similes
and that Adam was God's versifier

Pied

I was born with ink in my veins
and I teethed on grandfather's stories
of rambunctious bears and peregrinating
pigs who always came
in triplicate, and I don't remember
when I first heard a rhyme
chime, but something seethed
inside me, waiting to be
released, to be eased
in the pied precincts of a poem.

Dream

You interrupt my dream of you
in all your lyrical loveliness,
and I am doubly blessed,
having you in the sweet desmesnes
of my sleep then again
when I wake to celebrate the miracle
of our coupled love.

Chrysalid

O the artful girls
of Canatara, unfurling
fresh-breasted upon
its glistening sands, and the bashful
boys of Canatara eye
them warily, beyond
the scope of hope, and the Heavenly
blue blaze of the Lake
and its leavening light ignite
something akin
to lust within their newly-
gendered, just-out-of-
the-chrysalid hearts, all
thought of tender contact
lost in the misfiring
of desire.

Bloom

For Anne, in loving memory,
　with a nod to John B. Lee

When your heart no longer
hearkened and you left me
to grieve alone, I forgave you
your absence, undarkened
by the days I strove to fill
with thoughts of what we shared
before your abrupt sundering,
and in these rooms now
emptied of you, I still
remember a love that bloomed
in the bone.

Stalwart

As I was young and yearning
in the green Eden of grand-
father's lawn, I rose
with the sun's rising into morning
each dazzling day
and let a village envowell me,
whispering into my learning ear
the poem of home, and I
was hugged whole by a blue-
fuelled Lake and a jewelled
River and I was pulled
like a moon-tugged tide
to the brink of my word-turning
tongue and stanzas grew
like slow roses from the ink
of my blood: stalwart and true.

Allure

When God the Almighty
made Eve out of a random
rib to stroll with Adam
in tandem through the Garden
that never saw a spade,
the latter kept his gaze
upon the mums and daisies,
assured that Eve's allure
was sacrilege, and she,
to get even, took one
belligerent bite.

Tactile

For John B. Lee

We wade bare-breasted
into Huron's chilled blue
waves and, breathing froth
as they crest and tumble into
themselves, they lick
at the shore-wide sand
like tactile tongues, and we feel
in the undulance of the undertow
the pull of moon-tugged
tides and the world's ruthless
will, and we dive in
anyway, content to be flung
afloat, to batten down
on buoyancy, to be fractured
by a June-juiced sun.

Time's Tick

On a sun-strummed September
morning we abandon our summer
cocoons and hit the high
road for school, passing
Leckie's farm where Holsteins
graze lazily and shorthorns
remember themselves
and on past Gunn's place
where hogs wallow like hippos
with snouts in the snuffling mud
and the pasture where Grace grips
her stallion with incising thighs
and the hawthorn hedge where this
year's colt burgeons
his brand-new erection
(and the girls blush lushly
and the boys sing inside)
and in the haze ahead
sits the brick-coat
box we will inhabit
until the sprouting of Spring
releases us and I shout
for the sheer joy of titillating
Time's tick.

Moonless

For Anne in loving memory

I wake from a troubled sleep
into the delicate dome of the dark,
and outside the window
of this room the night
is moonless in a sky stippled
with stars, and I reach out
for the warm wealth of you
and find you gone into a
deeper darkness, and I long
to hear once again
the low lilt of your voice
and rejoice in the tender tilt
of your glance and know that some-
where beyond the heft
of Heaven you have found a home.

Horizon

And here I am stalking
the streets I roved over
when I was young enough
to know better, and throve
in a village that envowelled me,
where I found my Muse and began
iambicizing under
her enthused tutelage
and poems flowed like ribald
roses exploding into bloom,
and I felt like the Bard walking
blind into any horizon.

Quip

"There's no sin in innocence,"
quipped the Reverend Bell,
but did he see the ruby-
lipped girls of the Point
summering their thighs on Canatara
or the boys, playing the odds,
ogling the merchandise,
while far away where the sky
and lake fraternize
and where the dark gods conspire,
a rogue wave arises
serpentine and breaks
upon the soft shore
of the world.

Gist

We take turns running through
Grandpa's whirligig,
and we stare at Shirley's bare-
legged leap over the
skin-caressing spray,
rounded off by a cartwheel,
all effortless ankle
and sly thigh and wistful
grin, and when we meet
naked eye to eye,
I begin to suspect that girls
may be the keepers of something
secret in the world, in the gist
of its intricacy

Unbidden

I watch the Widow Bray
floating through her flowers,
pausing here and there
to dote upon a daffodil,
then praising a daisy,
and like Gaia thriving in her Grecian
garden, she waits patiently
for joy to arrive, unbidden.

Mettle

In the sultriest of seasons we gather
in Hendrie's abandoned coop
for some adult entertainment,
and when Joanne pulls down
her panties, we do more
than glance with lustful surprise
at the puckered petal squeezed
between her thighs, and I feel
like Lancelot going for the Grail
and waiting for the world to test
my mettle.

Ajar

On Christmas Eve the snows
come down in velvet volumes
upon eave and sill, hushing
the house where I lay abed
dreaming of reindeer with crimson
noses and Santa swaying
in his sleigh, and somewhere
beyond the Evening Star,
undimmed by distance,
a babe awakes and sets
the welcoming world ajar.

Galahad

For Anne in loving memory

For fifty-seven years
we rode the same rail,
shared a bed and breakfast
and woke afloat in one
another's arms, and you made me
feel like Galahad going
for the Grail or Abelard pursuing
Heloise with billet-doux
or St. George slaying dragons
for his lady, and even now
with you asleep somewhere
above Heaven's halo,
I dream you alive and thriving,
your face forever in the mirror
of my mind, aglow with the gift
of your irreplaceable, leavening
love.

Romance

They said it was just puppy
love, but what right
did "they" have to tell
the world what romance is?
After all, when we strolled
hand-in-glove or called
each other "dear"
or traded soulful glances,
I didn't know down from up
or if the moon still whirled
in its oracular orbit, but nothing
really mattered except
the feeling we shared: of sheer
unjaded delight.

Lots

When the summer sun goes down
in a haloed haze, we gather
beneath its amber glow,
and it's hide-and-go-seek
as we shrink into the umber oval
where the dark lurks under
the moon's lunatic light
and a sky inked with stippling
stars and do not care
that somewhere in the universe
the baffled gods draw lots
and laugh.

Forge

O the gorgeous girls of Canatara
in their one-piece suits,
curled on the sizzling sand
with their brand-new breasts
and the tender tuck between
their thighs while the bashful boys,
lashed by lust in the forge
of their desire, try their luck,
eyes upon the puckered prize,
saluting the day their God
bi-gendered the world.

Elixir

The aging poet takes the stage,
teeters and yaws on the lectern
for an immemorable moment,
fixes his bardic eye
upon the audience, sweetens
them with a smile, opens
his slim volume of verse
and begins to read in a baritone's
rumble the poems he's rehearsed
a hundred times in his head,
pausing to register a rhyme,
a lilting alliteration
or a nimble turn of phrase
before falling skillfully
silent, waiting for the elixir
of applause.

Abed

When I was just five,
I lay abed with measles
with the blinds discreetly drawn
and my mother tip-toeing
in every hour or so
and speaking in whispers as if
she spoke too loudly
I might break, and in my fever-
dreams the windows were bent
like Apollo's bow and the blinds
shivered as if buffed by a breeze
and I thought a lot about the gleam
in God's eye and what
it would be like to be
unalive.

Unalloyed
For Tom

You and I angling
on Cameron, doing our best
to outwit a fish,
dangling worms like manna
before the lidless finned-
swimmers combing the blue
fathom below, while we sit
in quiet companionship
as the afternoon drifts by
like a summertime snooze
and we are hugged on all
sides by birch and spruce
and fir as old as Adam
in Eden when the world was new
and we were just a dream
in God's abiding eye
and the tug of love was as unalloyed
as ours.

Night Terrors

Under Mara's lamp
and a stark sky embroidered
with stars and the moon's amplitude,
we ventured beyond the gaseous
glow into shadows shrouding us
from the unerring eye of the one
we designated "It," and we huddled
there witting and waiting
for the "All free" to echo
through the voluminous void
above and release us from the
night terrors plundering
our blood.

Antedeluvian

These dunes are older than
Methuselah's muse, their fluted
flumes soothed silken
by myriad on-shore breezes,
and I can see them still,
marinated by moonlight
or softened in the sun's bloom,
and I dream of the Attawandaron
coming here in the morning
of the world to read the runes
of their gods, bathe in Huron's
redeeming waters and lay
their bodies down on Canatara's
antediluvian sands.

Dance
For Sandra Grocott Gamble

It was only a summer romance
but you were the first girl
to see something in me
I never knew I had
and when you curled my hand
in the pleasing ease of your own,
I took it gadding through
the neigbourhood and, no
no longer lonely, I felt
my heart hum as one
by one curtains were drawn
askew to let us pass,
a lad and his lass, and I thought
even then I finally knew
what love was and what
it was like to dance inside.

Tinged

September 6, 1949

On that September morning
the sun rose on the hazed
horizon like glazed gold
and we set forth like Heracles
harrowing the apples of the Hesperides
with the song of beginnings inside us,
and we passed bedewed pastures
where Holsteins grazed lazily
and Leckie's fallow where Grace
galloped her stallion in the vise
of her thighs and on to the hawthorn
hedge fringed by wild
mustard and passed the field
where the callow colt cantered
with his eminent erection that sent
the girls wriggling with giggles
and as we drew abreast
of the schoolhouse we trusted
that this year our bi-gendered
lives would once again
be tinged with tenderness.

Hill

We had only one hill
in my village: where the Bridge
rose to its cantilevered leap
above the River and when
the snows came, we spent
our days on its slick slope,
our toboggans teasing the breeze
and leapfrogging over dried
weeds and rusted bulrushes
onto the glazed glide of the Marsh,
and we carried on, fancy-free
till the gloaming gathered us home,
where hope lived and love
abided.

Plot

God fashioned Adam out of dust
and made him in flesh and blood
with just enough male
machinery and then drew
Eve out of an extra rib,
complete with mammaries, womb
and uterine needs, then
dropped them into Eden where sex
was interdicted (even
the wisteria bloomed without
aid of pistil or stamen),
and so, the prudent pair
spent their days admiring
the scenery until Eve's
grapple with an apple and in-
sinuating serpents left
the couple rudely nude
with fig leaves abaft,
newly besotted and thus
upsetting their Maker's
pristine plotting.

Meandering
Point Edward: 1948

I took a day to look for
the "point," meandering along
Canatara's sinuous curves
all the way to the blue
profusion of the Lake scything
the River, and tracing the shore-
line, bent like a scimitar,
and on to Sarnia Bay's
silken swerve and home
again to Alexandra Ave
and grandfather's lawn
where the twinned Manitoba
maples loitered in the leaf-
breathing breeze and lilacs
bloomed in lavender light
and I was resigned to a
pointless village, but one
hugged by artful arcs
and quaint quarter-moons:
stapled on my heart.

Barelegged

O the barelegged girls
of Canatara! How we gawked
at them curled in their loveliness,
their-one-piece suits
and the prize between their thighs
upon the dimple of a dune –
and when they gave us the oestral
eye, we felt our young
stalks rising and crowing
to the moon.

Rupture

Adam was the first versifier,
naming the flora and fauna
of the garden, and when Eve
unribbed, he sang her similes
in effortless iambic and adorned
her in garlands of gardenias,
and all went well until
Eve waylaid an apple,
and, rudely nude, they were free
to bed and wed, but God
in his fury ruptured their nuptials.

Heaven

That summer when I was almost
eleven, we congregated
in Hendrie's disused coop
and Jo-Anne offered to show us
her "bum," but I was struck
dumb by the cozy cleft
where her thighs sighed,
and when she asked me to show
her "mine," I blushed like a
ravished rose and she grinned
all the way from here
to Heaven.

Breakers

For Anne in loving memory

Grief comes in waves
like breakers combing Canatara
and just when the last tear
relents, I find myself
roaming from room to empty
room, seeking your presence
(a glance recalled, the surprise
of some delight in your eyes,
the bright bloom of a smile)
and like the lone lingering
leaf on an autumn elm,
I will remember the breath
of an April breeze and the love
we shared that only Death
could cleave.

Puzzled

The Revered Bell, coming
home to a dark house,
smelled gas and, unalarmed
but puzzled, lit a match
and one minute he was in his vestibule
and another he wasn't, and when
he woke on his side lawn
unharmed, he could hear
a voice saying "Thank
God you're Presbyterian."

Promethean
With a nod to Walt Whitman

When lilacs bloomed last
in grandfather's yard
in their purple profusions, he was
still alive with the light
of living in his eyes, and me
just eight, prizing
those Saturday morning
workshops, watching him
cradle the lathe with fingers
as supple as Michelangelo's
upon his Pièta, and later
in the afternoon mowing
the back forty with sunlight
bathing his Promethean brow,
and I knew even then
that lilacs lose their lavender
while in my heart the nub
of love was still aborning.

Singing

O the girls of Canatara
lay their budding bloom-
thighed bodies along
its sinuous sands in one-
piece suits clinging
to their coy curvatures,
and when they start stretching
like yawning kittens, the boys,
suddenly smitten, feel
a tug in the blood, and when
one of the ogled gives them
the nod, something goes
singing inside.

Shy

O Nancy Mara! I see you
still on Canatara's dreaming
beach in your one-piece
suit cradling your curves
and you do not seem to mind
the rogue ogling of your shy
thighs, licked lovingly
by the Lake's undulance, but we
were young, rinsed by innocence
and new to the ticklish trick
of romance.

Communion

For Tom

Once again Tom
and I fishing on Cameron,
its mirrored surface as blue
as a morning glory seared
by sun and we let our lines
play out in lazy loops
and wait for the plug's splash
like a wistful whisper as we try
to dupe whatever finned
swimmer lurks below
while an afternoon slips by
and no words are needed
between us and the sky
for love is this quiet
unurgent communion.

Wonder

O what a village I was born to!
hugged by a Lake as blue
as a heron's wing stunned
by sunlight and a River
with a current as cunning as a
moon-tugged tide,
and I rose each morning
and strode its dew-lashed
streets and alleyways
like a pilgrim his progress,
to the tune of a bullfrog's
throttled song, and I reckoned
its runes for stories and plots
and drew its Dickensian denizens
into the precincts of a poem:
I drowned in its tantalizing tillage
and rode off in any direction,
my eyes widened by wonder.

Basso

For Anne in loving memory

O how you loved Robson,
that deep basso
like the low tones of a trombone
or a loose-tuned tuba,
singing "Shenandoah"
from the witting well of his soul,
and we listened together, letting
the music rumble and reverberate
until we drew as close
as any lovers passing
the time in the lucid glow
of their wedding night.

Salute

It was that July in Hendrie's
hen-house when Jo-Anne
did the hula-hula
dance and for an encore
dropped her pants, exposing
the sloe rosebud
hugged by her thighs, and we stared
at the mute wonder of it
before we came erect,
juggled our jewels and saluted.

Bone

For Tom

You and I frolicking
in the shallows of Cameron Lake
as sleek as dolphins in their sea-
warm surround and below
the granite is as old as Adam
elementary in Eden and we are
enwombed by birch
and spruce reflected in the lucid
blue element where finned
perch peregrinate and behemoth
bass cruise alone
and how much of that cold-
blooded world, how much
of History's mists or the
moon-slaked Mesozoic
touches us, bruises us
to the bone?

Womb

The Widow Bray, daughter
of Demeter, waters her roses
and watches everything
that grows bloom:
daffodils and daisies galore,
peonies and poppies asleep
in the sun, and her tiny
clap-board house
is bee-deep in petals
and sits in the centre of the town
she loves like a groomed womb.

Demesnes
Point Edward 1948

As I walked out upon
the morning of my village as green
as the keen demesnes of Eden
and the lifting mists exposed
the sun above First Bush
like a blown rose and my streets
were leavened with its light and I met
up with Wiz and Bones
and Butch and we played away
the summer's day on Canatara's
pristine beach where self-
erasing wavelets tongued
the sifted sand and we gave
no thought to when
or why under the sky's
innocent arc or God's
ingenious plotting in His high
Heaven for we were young
and the world was willing.

Inside

Curly-haired Shirley
doing the can-can
on grandfather's lawn,
strutting her stuff and flinging
her lovely long legs
so high wide and handsome
we burst into prolonged applause
and Shirley grins her little-
girl grin as if
to say, "Seen enough?"
that leaves us singing inside.

Romance

They said it was just puppy
love, but what right
did "they" have to tell
the world what romance is?
After all, when we strolled
hand-in-glove or called
each other "dear"
or traded soulful glances,
I didn't know down from up
or if the moon still whirled
in its oracular orbit, but nothing
really mattered except
the feeling we shared: of sheer
unjaded delight.

Precambrian: Cyprus Lake

For Tom in loving memory

Tom and I pole
our way through the blue
isthmus that keeps our lakes
from hugging, where bullfrogs
plop from lily-pads
basted with bloom, and we debouch
into Cyprus with the morning sun
gleaming the lake pristine
and we drop our baited lines
into the dark dells below
and wait for the first terse
tug, and later on
in the soft sift of the afternoon
we stroll through the woods
to the north, where butterflies
flutter on wobbled wings
and orchids lie in shy
disguise and a rattler seesaws
across our path and blue
jays natter in the breeze
and we step at last free
of our shadows and come face
to face with the great "Grotto"
gouged out of Precambrian cliff
and we look at one another
as if for the first time,
our love sealed by silence,
our thoughts aloft with the gods
who dreamed such a land.

Time's Tick

On a sun-strummed September
morning we abandon our summer
cocoons and hit the high
road for school, passing
Leckie's farm where Holsteins
graze lazily and shorthorns
remember themselves
and on past Gunn's place
where hogs wallow like hippos
with snouts in the snuffling mud
and the pasture where Grace grips
her stallion with incising thighs
and the hawthorn hedge where this
year's colt burgeons
his brand-new erection
(and the girls blush lushly
and the boys sing inside)
and in the haze ahead
sits the brick-coat
box we will inhabit
until the sprouting of Spring
releases us and I shout
for the sheer joy of titillating
Time's tick.

Oval

Under the amber oval
of Mara's lamp and all
along Monck Street,
lavished by moonlight,
we play our ritual game,
and Nancy and I contrive
to share a shimmer of shadow
and for a lucid moment
we do a duo's dance
and I, no Lancelot,
espy a careless thigh
and harbour thoughts of ravishment.

Chum

When Marilyn, my chum from school,
in the first bloom of her girl-
hood (with curls as wisped
as winter wheat), sauntered
past the hired hand
and me, the latter thumbed
his crotch, grinned and said,
"Now ain't that a sweet piece!"
and I wondered what part
of her he meant and what
made it sweet.

Legacy

The widow Bray stands
there alone, bee-
deep in her tenderly-groomed
garden (with poppies bleeding
scarlet, roses as red
as a bride's blush and violets
as lush as lavender), watches
the drones, pulsing with pollen,
do their dizzying dance
to apprise the hive of her blossoms'
whereabouts, and thrives
in her flowered bower like a
bloom-inducing wizard
despite the legacy of her loss.

Wish

My Dad and I fishing
on Mitchell's Bay, and I watch
in awe at the lazy, lofted
loop of his plug and its soft
plop on the weed-rich
shallow and when a pike
as big as a barnacled barracuda
strikes, he sets the hook
with an infinitesimal tug
and waits for the finned wriggler
to break the surface, its muscling
arc bent like Robin's bow,
defying the grasp of gravity,
but the fight is over, the game
won, and my father grins
at me as if to say,
'That's how it's done!"
and I wish the day would last
forever.

Adroit

For Tom in loving memory

On amber afternoons
Tom and I cavorted
in Cameron's shimmering shallows
like blue-finned dolphins
delighted with their own adroit
gymnastics, and we took turns
ducking under like cruising
loons, and Tom gave me
a gargantuan grin, as if
to say, "Such days
are a gift from the gods and we
are here, anointed," and I felt
a tug of love so strong
I wanted to hug him whole
and go perambulating to the moon.

Small Pleasures

John B. Lee

as always, for Cathy

In the Smallest Disturbance of Earth

all the poppy requires
for germination
is the smallest disturbance of earth
as with the slightest agitation of soil
its black and nearly invisible seed
will break open to life
like breath on crimson embers
blooming into flame out of warm grey ash

I remember being there
on the golden edge
of a wheat field ripening
in Roman ruins of Mediolanum
how the proud rust-red glory
of its flower
growing wild in rural France
bled into blue sky rising above the grain
coming out of fertile ground
by the broken terracotta
and the time-buried road
of an abandoned dig

what was considered there
a less-than-important remnant
of our archeological past
old wine cellars and dry wells
of a dead city
lost in the anaphrodesia
of cracked stone
and shattered amphora
with its thirst for burgundy
in shards of clay
like a ghostly stain from the kiss of desire
in the briefest season
of a single gloaming
or the slow-to-wake passing of dawn
we who remember heaven's ephemera
cry out from the wonder of the womb
cry out from each fragile generation
of all living things
given over
to birdsong and daylight

what's bone in the palm line of science
what's bone to the silence of night

Chorus Frogs Singing of Spring

on the bend in the trail from below
he hears how the rising choir
of chorus frogs
are singing
their water song
from the shallow swamp
among the broken reeds
and cattails of Silver Lake
as it is
with the first warming
of April
they set forth
emerging from thaw in the cracked open earth
like soft-bellied sculptures
breaking forth from the muds
of creation
and then milting the mirror
of the shivering sky
amphibian vandals of still surfaces
shimmering with the luxuriant and fertile murk

this is the sexual green
of algaeform pools
primordial ovum
and the living and come-to-life
punctuation born in inky throbs
that stop the breath of the walker
knowing he must earn
his next step before
moving forward and into the glory

It Wasn't Always This Way

here at my desk
writing in the living smoulder
of lake flies
watching the clear air thickening
on this early-May morning
with the saw sound
of the mid-spring first flight and tumble
of these mouthless midges
blackening the sill
in doomed snags
like small mending
in tattered thread
wing-tired and dying tangles
like breath in whiskers
and the lean-in-close for listening
to small-haired words
they are mating
in a quick fizz of lust
a lascivious rush
of ash in flight away from fire
they bead upon single strands
of webbing
and break with beauty
like tattered gauze
spidering down the casement
of this house
and they also float where they fall
into rain water
that remains
for the lifting of the light
in evaporate catches
and they drown there in tiny fatigues

for what sky desires
of the mirrors it holds
at this very moment invisible made more invisible
and glancing off into come-close distance
between soaking in and rising up
they become the dregs of nature
the dross of silt and settle

… and he says of the arrival
four hundred years ago of Dollier and Galinée

      it wasn't always this way

imagine the French
in their birch-bark canoes
paddling into the winter sheltering
of this Canadian paradise
where the wild grape thrives
and the bear meat
hisses on a makeshift spit
and they survive the perilous whiteness
of the soft-hearted wilderness

dear reader from the future
dream also of me
drinking this coffee
with its well of tiny flies
as I inhabit the vanishing into fog of your

      once upon a time

Wonder-filled

I walk the trail
at the cock's crow of morning
and am
wonder-filled
by the roostering of enthusiasm for new light
what then
is the fragrance of desire
to me
but the spirit's perfume
of mud
and the thumbnail
odour of juniper berry
that breaks open
like the uncapping of ceiled gin
and the blue-green seeping
aromas of tree seed
and the flag-rip sounds
of the earth
with its silken exhale
at the zenith of a man-made tower
what is it
I am learning
from the acorn hatching at my feet
doffing its cap in the dirt
or the deadfall fungus
given a second chance
in the fertile remainder
of rotting away at heartwood

and the ripening stream
that hungers for rain
to be loblolly enough
in this becoming the silt
in a clay bed descending
to where the black pond of a shining sky
lowers its voice tumbling down in a foamy rush
at the bridge

all heaven
is briefly burning
in blue fuel
and the ardor of bird song
waking

if I pause in my stride
and dare to listen
Wordsworth whispers
… go on, continue
step lively enough to be still
keep pace with the soul
and the mind will teach
and the body will learn
and the earth will be present within …

Morning Song

there, lying in the grass
just beyond the chain link's
tessellated wire-shadow falling
like a net upon green water
at the garden's edge
the evidence of midnight feasting
resident in a whirl of feathers uplifted by a draft
to shape the last gestalt
of moonlit murder
within the ghost flight of an absent breath
blue beauty torn to silence
like the voiceless buoyancy
of vanishing mist
what clarifies the talon
and sharpens the claws of dawn
but the predatory darkness
gyring out of light-pierced heaven
making the earth
sniff-worthy to my little dog
finding hints and traces
of crimson passion
redolent from the dreamer's hour
while the once radiant singer
gave up its body
to this, the quietest of morning songs

if I am not here, then why …

if I am not here
to catch and hold
the delicate rings
rising in radiant
undulations
under the rain
that thrills
the still pond
with shivering O's
those briefest of waves
echoing outward
in shining black circles
that seem
to comfort the calm waters
like the slow subsidence
of weeping
then why …

this cognition
this apprehension
of ephemeral
mutability in wet reflection
on the shimmering black surface
of a secondary forest
and heaven's
dark emulsion
this silt-burdened
child of cloud-mothered life
caressed by weather

and the departing sorrow of late-morning storm
is just now
healed by light easing in strands
through the grey lux
of an overcast
at the hour of let up

this lull
that wants one mind's homage
longing to find a sufficient
and attentive
consciousness
an honouring solitude
someone to linger
and become
reverent and vigilant witness
of unlasting things
lest we forget
the slipping away
of largess and are
as it were
with the dying out of a fire
into cold ash, for
the limb that cannot hold the leaf
is wintering away into cynical shade
much like the intelligence of man – bereft

For All His Dark Dreaming

though I yearn to forget
much memory remains
as remembered regret
like the shadow of rock
in water
oh the shadow of rock
on water
one lovely ephemera
of the painterly
sun-blue day
they shine on the surface
as shadow play
turning on the smallest of words
in and on and under
as unseen thoughts
might flicker
in peril from pain
of the time-troubled mind
a secret betrayed
by the turn of the mouth
its border
vermilion as a gravestone kiss
the lingering osculation of red moss
and black lichen
or in those sad
eyes, the brow furrowed
lashes blinking
at lies

but the rock-shadowed water
encircles the shale
and swallows the slate
of the pier
invisible island - the jetty is drowned
and the lake
enthralls the sailor's heart
as lagan sunk in its bed
for all his dark dreaming
he wakes
with a mouth full of sand

The Bee in the Blossoming Crab

yesterday's lake
not the same as today's
with the surface
a blue shiver of light
on the shimmering bay
a calm agitation
of an offshore breeze
on Thursday last's unlasting afternoon
the breakwall roared
in the high dudgeon
of angry water
where the stones of the pier
rose and fell to be seen and unseen
like the half-drowned spine
of a great primordial beast
a breathless leviathan shale
lashing its dying tail
in the coming and going away
of grey waves
a wet line of foam
slapping the earth
with an all-gathering
indignation
of a worry enraged
a goddess of ire
in angry discord
with hard-edged heights
longing to climb
the dampening crags of broken clay

the cross crests and cross troughs
roiling to double
their worth
and dulling the sun
to a valueless brown
like the lapse-in-time
rusting of steel

all sound
the shunting of trains
or the crashing of glass
come to whispering
now and now against   now

and I'm the same man
soaked to the soul
like sweat in old felt
when the mutable life of the world
might still amaze the mind with a bee
in a blossoming crab

Ode to an Oriole Feeding
Upon an Orange Outside my Window

the oriole lands and sups
and seems a lazy flame
slow burning from the broken orange
it serves the soul
upon the wheel of fruit
like calcium on fire
in the golden candle of the mind
it grips the light
as brilliant feathers will
when they are brightened from within
and there
it feeds upon the citrus gills
the pulp fanned open in a circumference
cupped round by zest
and like my mother's
homemade marmalade
come silver-spooned
into a breakfast bowl
might also
bring my father
from the barn's divine
hay-heavened mow

the rind in jam jars
proves the source as bittersweet
the maker and the made
are both divine in this
and memory's a fault
that cannot make it real

what's in the nest next door
hangs in a woven home
a sacred house that swings upon the wind

Ideas of Ideal Beauty

two grackles
are flacking in the grass, their wings
like turbulent waters breaking over stone
and it is spring
when the boundaries
of the body
are broken open
by fire in the fuel within their hollow bones
like a hot disturbance
of crimson kindling
collapsing inward
as the red flower
catches and blooms in brilliant
fevers of creation
while midges smoulder on the alter of a shrub
as it is also with the uplifting of smoke
from the fertile smudge pots
of human breath in forest moss
a coupling of sparrows
a frenzied allegory of grey squirrels
leaping and racing and rushing together
in the fecund acrobatics
of April
tails throbbing and threading through branches
of maple   branches of oak
tipped in bud bursting into
the beautiful blue amplitude
of a sun-warmed morning

make heaven the mistress
of true longing
in every nest and bower
every hutch
and stall
it's lambing in the meadow
and calving in the straw
there's work enough in green cathedral of every leaf
to bring honey to the hive
that's shaking out of slumber
and Gaia is walking in her gardens
lost in the middle pages of her most holy book
the one concerning glory
not of dazzling starlight but of the gentler movements
in the more luminous milk light of the moon
In the Bountiful Absence of Everything

wild yellow coneflowers
present themselves
like old buttons
to a museum of sunlight
in tatters
calling out by wind-fastened
batches
to the honey-headed drones
their pollen baskets
furred with the slow result
of flower dancing
they crawl and tumble

clumsy like the thumb's permission
unlatching the dust
of ghost lovers
and the antique memory
of lost bodies
heaving on the breast
of this day
what weeps in the comb
in the sweet hexagrams
of the hive
the sticky viscosity
of the much remembered
meadow
of this particular summer morning
that now
in memory moves this pen
the same moment
tracing the eye
that follows the ink
in the bountiful absence of everything

This Then

this then
is for those who cannot see
beyond the chalk
for there
in my yard
stands a stunted tree
one branch of lonesome leafing
sending out
an arm of bloom in spring
like a child
with a fistful of stolen flowers
the joyful offering of seedbed larceny
and there it is delighting
with its nosegay
of a single season
every one its last
to seem uprooted
from the timberline
the krummholz of a crippling wind
one foot in winter
even as the clock strikes June
and if we refuse the tangled roots
their waterline
we also live in equal perils
of a common sun
the moonlight
silvering the gilded lake
caresses every bony branch
and hangs its lamp within

the twisted phylum of the heartwood
earth to sky
and if there's sacred action in the stars
all precious monuments find solace
in the fractured beauty
where it breaks blue light

It Might Have Been Beautiful

it might have been beautiful
this morning invasion
a family of five
there at the chairs and table
on the back deck
a black-masked mother
and her four kits
the sow - a slow involvement
of rock and waddle
her sharp-nosed features
her fine-fingered hands
the whiskery faces
and ringed-tails throbbing
but I remembered
how my cousin Ted's farm dog Clarence
had been blinded in one eye
by a polecat altercation
I'd heard
how a raccoon boar
nesting all winter in a neighbour's attic
had clawed its way
out through the roof
from the inside
emerging as though born through the shingles of spring
and so
I resolved to have them gone
at first
tapping the glass on the door
to get their attention
but rather than startlement

I received
the shambling curiosity
of five confident thieves
entitled interlopers stealing the day
with a wild refusing
and so I came out clapping
but rather than rush
they simply turned
two climbing the close-at-hand
big leafed Norwegian Maple
three crossing the yard to the garden
allowing me the brave illusion
of ownership and power
as they mastered the fence
walking the spine like the trailing of fingers

how rare in daylight
these nocturnal trash raiders
their sharp features drenched in scraps
dripping with midnight hunger
and the loud tin-can tumult
their amber eyes blazing in darkness
me - in their minds
a momentary inconvenience
something to consider and dismiss
while crossing the stream they are dreaming
like clouds over moonlight

As Was His Nature

as was his nature
my small Jack Russell dog - the one my good friend
calls the little gentleman
coming out of the sky on the hill to the shore of the bay
raced down the last of the stairs with a single purpose –
to flush the fledgling grackle he'd spotted
from the shadows of the breakwall –
so up it flew in startled response
then fell from the rim of the earth
and then tumbled downward
dropping into the clutches of the ugly roil of the lake
the doomed bird flacking its ragged wings
like black flags tattered on the water top
as it sank to the bone of its breast
in the crest of an angry wave
to be soaked by the weight of impossible flight
where it clung to its feathers in foam
like over-washed wool

and I watched in helpless adoration
as in desperate sorrow it gulped
taking death in great open-beaked swallows
five or six full thirsty sobs
and just as it drowned and was dying
one energetic amplitude of wind-worried water
lifted it out of the looming swell
then dashed the small nut of its skull
against rusty corrugations of iron
and so finished its work as the bead of an eye

went wide to the world and then narrow
till it shut on a stunned squint and lay where it sank
no longer alive
its body awash in grey darkness
as though tugged by a thread from below

and my sweet companion
my small dog Sarge
all the while barking and barking
at the loud and insouciant lake

Something Dead in the Sun

in the garden walk
beside the house
in passing
I notice
the fragrant waft of putrefaction
rising from the earth
and I know
though I cannot fix the exact sorrow
of its whereabouts
there is something dead in the sun
a pungent perfume
of rotting flesh
interweaving with
the winey over-ripening
of fallen apples
how they vanish in the grass
like the melt away
of light-warmed ice
the green release of red
transformed to brown
the lazy monument
of measured wind-weight
on a swaying branch
and then the lassitude
of autumn hands
the fog that plucks the stem
like weather ghosts

but there
the sick-sweet rose
and there the other vast aromas
mapped by wasps
and long-tongued butterflies drawn down
through fluxing thermals
like the decorous rearranging
of a party flounce of stiffened silk that won't stay put

I stop
and give the poverty of human noses
this task of mind
and there I spy
unseen for days
the squirrel corpse
flat to the bed
where oleogustus
sours the time-greased bones
with leathery tufts of seed-grey fur
like the unshaping of a half-drawn thing
an vivid incompletion
like the ground heave of a flooded grave

a childhood on the farm
familiar with dog loss
and the winter scraps
of cat and calf
almost prepares the shovel face
and shallow hole
to hold the dream count
of an over-quiet stone

The First Great Dying

two-hundred-and-fifty million years ago
or so the fossil record shows
there occurred on earth
what scientists believe
to have been
the first great dying
in the speciation of toxic rain
with acid oceans
asphyxiating life
in all its blue-green glory
gone the grey of plant-imprinted stone
long before
the thunder lizards
last lifted their three-horned heads
in dead-skull stupefaction
among the feathered ferns
that perished in what
must have seemed eternal winter
as ice encumbered
the mountain-shouldered land
while naked strangers
forked the bridges
in drifting rivers of floating freeze

how long an afternoon
might seem then
to the ennui of dull hours
when an individual mind
is bored

by the slowness of passing time
and melancholy tedium
of a shadow clocking the day in ephemeral darkness
how then might church
or school
or the repetition of an overcast
give grim excitement
to the vapors
that drop grey sorrows on the lake
while foam-veiled waves
dash and dash and dash again
like water-spangled dancers
and are gone

A Ghost in the Spirit of Stone

who cares for the fossil
I've found in the library garden at noon
still bearing the shape
of the shell
in a stone
like a veil
on the face of the dead
a plaster-cast mask
of an African queen
Nefertiti of the Nile
the river that flows
through a book
the Biblical waters
of a Sunday-school mind
made real
as an apple is real
in the palm
and as time lives on in this grit
like clay on the edge
of a spade
or in memory hard
as old ice
my powerful thumbs
read the ribs of this rock
and are blind
as a hand in a glove
millennial bone
of a writer's regret

has a ghost for the ink
in the spirit of stone
this foggy caress
knows the heartbeat's my own
though the creature I hold
crawls out of the land
like the seed from a star in the earth

in light, the colour of creatures

for six-hundred-million years
thunder lizards
walked the ferny swamps
of Eden
and now we learn
they were not grey
but rather
iridescent as the blue-black
starlings feathering the light
and beaking the lawn
for seed

how they came painted
like the red-hind baboon
copulating in the road
and leaping onto the shining hood
of a cloth-top Thunderbird passing
through safari land
amusing a car full of laughing children
before stripping the chrome
and ripping the aerial out by the root
like a slender-stemmed silvery weed

we who are older are considering
the big blue metaphysical
wide-open thighs of heaven
in comet-creation and wonder
at the sudden cold ice-thickened world
its time-shocked planetary awe

like the paling away to white marble
of the armless,
the headless, the one-legged
stone statues of ancient Rome, fallen
to ruin
though they once blushed
like Caligula's naked sisters
stepping into glory
rising in vanishment
like the ghostly desires of fog
an all-caressing veil
of the soul as vapour
the body
as dust, the ashy patina
of the palm of death
drifting down from Vesuvius

oh amorous volcano
oh passionate tsunami rising like shadows in light
every fearful wind
the twisting of water
seeking the treeline, the mudslide
the wet sludge land-girdling river
carrying arms sunk to the wrist in
that waving away of lost towns
and doomed cities
Atlantis - her innocent dreamers
swallowed in silt

we who are the lovers
lying in the afterglow
of wildfire
still burning the bones
in divine interdiction
though the spine
cracks its seed in the embers
and heart blooms once again
in the scarified hand of the Lord
we still speak with voices of smoke
in the silent language of the lost

... see how dying draws a crowd

the young raccoon
came totter-walking to our lawn
it seemed to yearn
to lie down and die
for like a child
it may well have been crying
      sick, oh sick - in silence
so deep and real it fell upon all
like drifting smoke
with a gathering crowd
of neighbours
circling and speaking
in hushed tones - quiet, be quiet -
as with its small hands
in prayer it turned
a drab stone like the shell of a nut
as though it might solve
eternity in the fan fossil
of that millennial dross
and then
it curled on its tail
and slept
in the fever light
on the ailing green
softness of the all-receiving earth

what of dogs on leashes
and dogs in locked rooms
bragging at the closed door

this wild creature
wants shriving
in the lost-light apple blossoms
and bird song
grieving on the wing
for all the lonesome sorrows
in the oriole's orange-throated
hallelujahs
and in the ugly threnody
of the blue jay coughing
enough enough   and

it was done

oh see how dying draws a crowd
quilting the world into care-filled stitches
when the heart
falls free of the mind

The Wild and Lovely World

my wife coaxes me
to turn my head slowly
don't move now
she says
just look, lest you startle
the wild and lovely world
outside the window
as though a glance
might shape the yard
as hot light sometimes
withers green and dries away the rose

there are blue feathers
flashing, crimson wings
gone in a blink and brilliant
yellow angels of delight gone off and off

yet as the waking dreamer
dulls the room
with the consciousness
of ordinary morning
there's dove hunger
enough in the scatter seed
to satisfy
the sparrow brown
and crack-shelled ground
but want of colour
wounds the earth's ecru
all lively grey
remainders of winter's iridescent loss
drab singers flit

and strut and scratch
and seek
to please the mind
in multitudes

the timid garden brief with frost
the shining hoar that gilds the melting dew
where life is dying down

you are the warming of the chill
the open palm
that feeds the kill
the change that comes
with knowing
of the vacant hill

go name the woodcock
in the wood
go seek
the beaver in the gnaw
like broken match ends thick above the swamp
you bring about a noble silence
that longs to see you gone

Living Upside Down

a hapless squirrel
my wife has been pampering
for months
so it has become winter fat
on the calorie-rich birdseed
she leaves out there in the feeder in the garden
mostly intended as a source of all singing
on the boreal winds
of cruel-to-the-light-of-the-day mornings
come late in the year
a wild chattering
of ravenous creatures occupying the heights
of the leaf-naked maples
and bony-fingered white birches
in any event somehow he has slipped
into the wrought iron crotch of the hanger
so he's trapped and dangling by one leg
living upside down for hours
looking much like a decorative illustration
of the beasts of Eden
some folio verso of the lost creatures
of the fallen world
and I wonder if I told him
how in the mind of Einstein
he was suffering not from the green pull of the earth
but rather mostly from
the blue push of the invisible palm of the sky
how long in the dying of heaven
would he be consoled by the contemplation
of the fate of apples
knocking the forehead of Newton
with the knowledge of frost drop in the stem of the fruit
how long there then

till his last breath brought its final amazement
and after that the coldblooded taxidermy of time's great blackening
dispatching the heart's concern gone still as a stone
lodged deep in a patch of fur

oh but my life-loving wife
intervenes when she sees him
and she catches him up
in a double-knit hat
while he fights from within
biting the weave in every direction
still she lifts him out by his caught leg
disentangles his fury
as he lashes his tail
and throbs in the sheltering darkness
of her Canadian toque
and then she sets him free
and he races away to the thought of tomorrow's returning

Sweet Remembering

how differently the snow
adorns these various conifers
the cedar, the fir tree
and the pine
dressed out and draped in white
the black-branched
leafless oak
the broken kexes
and the yew
the shrubbery beset with cotton tufts
the hand refuses
to refine with shadow gloves
cold-shouldered apple boughs
ragged out in epaulettes of glaze
and there
above the picker's frosted sleeve
that leaves its ghost upon the watered bark
the ruined appetite
of winter clings in rotten beauty
bobbing on a broken wind
a season's stronger stem that will not yield
the heights

what drops
its chill among the needles
drifts like smoke-weight
to the earth
and pierced along the way
to cure particulars
in softened sweeps of discontinuous shapes
that dust the gravel
and then vanish
like powder from a lady's puff

all sweet remembering
is vanquished thus
though words might hold it
in a breath of ink
like darkness born in light

Merry Christmas

a holdover from the season of Yule
in through the scalding window glass
of January morning
came the sun
steeping the glaze
so a single beam
bent by the focal prism
of a bobble on the sill
a snow globe
magnifiying light
to a pinprick of heat
so it scorched
the faux oak grain of a nearby tabletop
with a black dot seared
like blight on a leaf
and a puff of smoke rose
off lacquer and veneer
as it is with the cozy combustion
of newsprint and kindling
this being the accidental optics
of an unintended experiment
from the mischief of physics and solar bloom

what fire makes available
when it leaps
from the woodlot to the tree line
like a red-breasted bird

from all wild quandaries
of every great disaster
from the conflagration of Troy
down to the smallest calamity of individual time
from one child
torturing a pismire
with the cruelest surmise
of a single lens
to Torquemada torching the heretic
with his most sanctimonious wrath
and the high priest Caiaphas and his
judgment of the Sanhedrin
all magnificent temples in flame
like the Coconut Grove

what's ashes to ashes
or dust to dust
when it's a question
not a statement

I might enquire of the singed ant
come briefly to cinders
the moment his armour whiskered with light
like a shimmering filament
in a bubble of candied glass
his last thought brilliant and burning…
ask all good men of Gomorrah
ask all doomed saints
every last hagiography
in the sacred history of humankind
why we find ourselves
searching forever for that which can never be found

Mostly the Snow

mostly the snow
that lies deep on the mantle
rising up to the windows
of the miniature
Victorian village
shining like glazed candy
in the firelight of Christmas
mostly the snow is taken from ticking torn
from stuffed toys ripped to shreds
by our Jack Russell Terrier
Sergeant and put to another purpose
every year my wife
sets out those decorative dwellings
the church and the library
the town hall
and the manse
where the parson
is surely breeding his whelp
for the hunting of foxes

and every year
the white snow deepens
and billows
up to the rooftops
up to the gables and spires
like clouds rolling in from the mountains
here a tuft of Aspirin wadding
there the cotton-throated teddy bear's result
grown slack in the neck and
ripped at the seams
and in the aftermath
of the festive season
when the town is boxed in the basement
the bookshelf remains dusted
like a cotton mill floor swept clean
after the lights have gone out
all over Liverpool
all over England

Admonition Against Injury

the snow lies blue upon the earth
the eaves
are fanged in ice
cold lingers
like the breath in death
that stirs
the broken thread of life
where winter
holds an aching hand upon the chest
like lovers who caress
the gone-still sparrow
of the human heart
what auguries of spring
there are
come singing
in the shadow's song
of light
undress this solitude
and see
where absence is an inch
of frozen tears
that melt
in lengthening
then shine
like temporary chandeliers

Islands Away from My Hand

I stand at the edge of the bay
and see
how the close-at-hand ice
resembles the scape of the moon
which seems waterless white
and pocked over with dust
that clings in the dips
and hollows
and scattering scree
rising through rubble
to a random berm of a cracked-back beast
imagine my footstep
in this tranquil freeze
I am the wolf
who in his thirst
comes sounding the lonesome hour
of solitary souls
in the thin-aired night
where the wilderness thrills
to be touched by an ambient howl
of silence and stars
I am walking alone
with Orion
whose quiverless bow
sings over the lake
like the white on a canvas
awaiting my brush
which is islands of ice away from my hand

On Viewing the Super Blood Wolf Moon I Contemplate the most frequently asked Google Lunar Question: Is the moon real?

last night
in the ultra-black heavens
of our very own
and most particular
January sky
into the otherwise dark cathedral
of a snow-blessed yard
we stepped out
onto the winter creak
of the deck boards
and looking up
through a divine network
of denuded branches
saw where the time-lapse eclipse
of a blood wolf moon
transformed its light
like the sanguinary marrow of life-soaked bone
and we felt
primeval wonder
ancestor awe
the slow amaze
of an ancient astonishment
as with a worshipful connection
to old-soul mythologies
we were there
among cave fires smouldering
on the inner walls
of a deep remember
where the breath of our silence
plumed in the boreal quiet
and was gone

Parable of the Mouse and the Owl

I was driving home
my car enclosed in the white claustrophobia
of a winter storm
my headlights stuffing
a luminous squall with angel-form
my mind threading
the slow squint of a winding road
as though lost on the narrow meander of a farm lane
I'm following the rocky outcrop
cut into the perilous contours
of the limestone escarpment
I'm auto-caught between an unforgiving guardrail
and the sheer face
of an ominous stone god
rising up and out of the earth looming over the lake
as though in judgment of all smaller things
my heart   like a runner's heart
my prayer   simply to exhale
to defeat the morbid
altitude   this slab shadow
              this death bringer
hovering as an opaque whirlwind
of indifferent darkness
doubled by a wet-feathered blizzard
and there in my path
fate has placed a full-stopped stranger
blocking the way
and both directions drop

down

for all my lonesome importuning
of divine intervention
this deus ex machina
becomes my circumstance

and there in that unloving cold
in that mouse and owl moment
I meet the plunging edge of everything
star-born and eventual
and on my own in the universe
I vanish looking up at the red claws of heaven
looking down on the shrinking hill

Alive

there is a certain amount of melting
makes things shine
butter, for instance
or the slow decline of wax retreating
in reflected fire
cold honey
crystal-white — when heated
seeps with new desire
thus remembering the once forgotten comb
the broken-open buzz
in hexagrams of the stolen hive
if lovers only knew, alive
the secret allocation
of the morning rose
the polished thigh that is the moon on waves
the fragrant trellis
of the apiary mind
we'd all be poets dancing our tongues
to tell the town
like bells
we'd find the common
concerns of every market square
within the sweet agora
of the marriage bed
but we are mostly
sometimes only where the beetle
eats away the leaf
to shadowloss
while day shade

drops green lace
upon the green below

and if I sing
as songbirds sing
of things I care to know

I'd sing the shape of snow
shrinking in the sun
turned briefly blue
in dietary warm
transform the winter yard
with childhood angels
falling free and wild
I'd make a fort
of heavy circles
where I'd wish …

for this

the strange isosceles
conceals the heart
transfigured
by divine events
like ecstasies of rain
the weedy headland
rising thick with life
a garden dreamer dreaming soul to soul

And time

the lake
where it swells and rises over the wall
has styled the iron rail
with strands of ice
like the braiding of soup
in an old man's beard

and it hangs
a wool wash of frozen water
from the crank of the come-along
and it's laundered the cogs
with a wet congeal
so they're greased
and hard-fat grey
so they stick to the teeth
that will not turn
to the will of the hand

with a cable
broken and frayed
with wire red-nasty in the flesh
spiked like a burr in the palm

above the missing stairs

and time
like a caught zipper
biting into the skin

And I, This Evident Man

the wind
like a ghost at the door
opens the house
to the voice of the world
both birdsong and
commerce at work
the human grumble of a loud machine
and the quiet response of the larch
and the lawn close-at-hand
the worm
measures hunger in rags of the lily
and the sparrow grows fat
on spilled seed
what the window says once
the screen utters twice
and the wind
gives a word to each leaf
the gravel
lies silent without me
ah   responding
impressions of past walking
the lifting and falling away of the sound
like bruises on apples
who think of the ripening sun
as they drop from the branch to the bruise
and yet
this evident man
he of invisible heart
this stranger from
memory's hold draws forth from the dark
it was I

who am hearing and
I who will hear
what was heard unremarked
and the mute ink of all large books
those resting nearby lexicons
wait somewhere for the thumb's surprise
or the accidental lapse in order
on the shelf
the spirit weight of old time
comes tumbling into out-of-reach phrases of dust

how hunger concerns
the fox-waking hour
while the coyote
breaks out of the gorse
and moonlit rock
speaks of cougars and lake-light
the language of gulls
oh I — from the silver ears of fishes
I from the bounty of waves
all tintinnabulations of water
ringing on this page — remember

At First Light

the wind
was shaking its fist
at the world
and the lake
was riled
with a wild indifferent
energetic roiling
of waves in foam

with my wife
asleep in a quiet room

what catches the earth
in a grip
of dream

grey heaven waking
and this breath of weather
sparrow-clawed
with life that clings
like filaments
of glowing heat
within the mind
red truth
reveals a covenant
between the darkness lost
at dawn
and the luminous darkness
gained by absent light

Hawberries on the Silver Lake Trail

what is the soul then
but a drift of mist reaching through
JBL

seeing red hawberries
in the silver light
of a winter sun
tree limbs glazed in ice
I am reminded
of candied fruit drawn shining
from liquid sugar
where the frozen blood
of wounded weather hangs
those crimson beads
clinging to the tip of the bone-thin branches
of the fire-sharp hawthorn
dangerous to the hand
yet lovely to the eye
in and through this lovesick garden
we follow the old carousal of familiar paths
leading from lost to lost
shaping the life of the day
with an almost-always-and-forever exhausted beauty

Still Water, Still Night

little insect
comes wing-singing
like an oriental aria
piercing the chiaroscuro
in the blood-hungry ugliness
of the woodlands

it comes
thriving into the red slap
the crimson smear
darning the thread hematoma
of hatched hair

on this most masculine arm
a lump leaver
wounding an itching inch
of anticoagulant dizziness

all morning it danced
over the sun-luminous leaf canopy
lifting a sprightly six-legged noise
like pulled-out mending
a snag in blue silk
small dragon of a fever-room sky
still-water demon
miasma of a green mirage

the sick sleeper in his winding sheet
enters the long night
that comes at noon

oh heavenly swarm
in the verdant delirium
of summer days
or in gloaming
at the loudest hour
of deep silence
in the blue-grey harmonious quiet
of shadow-cast dingle

you come
looming *little death bringer*
riding the stillness
like a saw cut stopping in wet air
a rip in the haze

where moon-monocled Divinity
looks down through ovipository evening
and sees both the best of His works
and the worst

The Lake in Storm

what the lake wants in storming
the wall
it will take
when   with the sledging of waves
it comes thundering in
forming the force of a watery punch
lifting like rot from a ripening red
in old iron
it wars on the hill
breaking the heart of the land
where with a
glutinous wash it erodes
at the warren
made steep as in fallback
of armies
abandoning death in retreat
in the trace of cold trash
its making a shore
in the drift of a ruining line

and like frost
it floats stone
rubbled like skulls
from the grave
capped in green
the ghost thought of shale
shaved away
where it breaks like old ice

and what is no longer there
comes to mind

as fathers of fathers
once sons of lost sons
become seasons of fields
under fields after fields
in the beautiful belly of seeds

The Vanishing

on the occasion
of the inexhaustible huff
of last season's late-spring storm
the lake rose
to the break of the wall
with water and ice
roiling and rolling
over the raised edge of the land
licking the crag and climbing the cliff
like the ravenous tongue
of a great beast
lapping raw bone
and this ominous weather
a thief of all it touched   took
stone and boat
shook broken chain
like a leviathan wild with rage
in frozen bonds
and one might call that morning
the vanishing for there
in the ghost ice glassing tall grass
there in the filthy berm
the cold fossil of what remained
what little was left
lay crafted in wet snow
and water-hardened ruination of things

the lock
like an insect in amber
the etched edges of rope fray
hawsers sunk to knots
in deep freeze

and it would be weeks
before softening
weeks until the warm sag
of shore trash
littering the hill
like the passing there
of a picnic reunion
unhappy evidence
of the appetites of ogres and ghouls

Unseen

she tells me
that blind children
will stand forever
by the mill in the late-autumn clearing
with their seed scattered palms
turned up and open to the sky
for receiving the birds when they come
lighting on the lifeline
the dark-eyed juncos
the black-capped chickadees
itching and pecking
almost weightless with wonder
they will crack
their beaks with a soft peck of hunger
like pen nibs writing the truth of a vanishing story
scribed on the soft flesh of the heel of the supplicant hand
then lifting off from below the pulse
blurring their wings gently
in a grey wash of air
they will trace pale veins
to the source
like a thread from a cave of the lost
for want of the grain they will call
from the red heart of the pine
from the blue flame
of the oak

from the white shelter
of late apples they will call
as angels cry from heaven
unseen by all others but them
in the faith loss of a long afternoon
they will stay and stay
open palmed
like the pods of weeds they will winter
in generations of generous darkness

"... the living things of the world are never far from water"

I watch a solitary grey squirrel
through the window
drinking from water
that carries his face
in small radiant arcs
as he laps the silver shiver
his tiny hands gripping
the rim of the bowl
his boy shoulders hunched
his pelt wrinkled like homespun
he tongues
liquid with a delicate pink
intrusion
as though he were saying
the word *thirst*
at this fingertip font
with the briefest pulse of a blessing
he seems grateful
for this and the seed drop
grateful for the shell
food in its frangible carapace
he cracks
along the fault line
what spills from the bench
in the garden
like broken-string pearls

I've seen him leap
risking the gaps
in thin-limbed shade

or is this a she-squirrel
nesting her kit in thatch
in the cross-hatched heights
of the willow

yesterday in Iceland
the citizens of that
once cold nation
mourned the death of a glacier
as with the weeping away
to a white blink
ten-thousand-year-old ice
died down to the size of a Canadian dime
a silver lozenge
that finally vanished
into the brown landscape
like sugar dissolving in tea

and though
the living things of the world
are never far from water

this droughty acquiescence
is also the dry well
of a widow's eye
holding her purse
to her breast
in the city

A Brief Encounter

walking my dog
in the darkness
I see a stray fox
trotting along the suburban street
where I live
as she
slips into the shelter
of hedges
a wild creature
braving the groomed cedar
she emerges, her shadow shape
sliding like the settle of silk
upon air
she eases like water
that pours
from a vase to a ewer
for the laving of hands
she knows
where she longs to be going
she's clicking her claws
on the ice of the road
like the coming of rain
upon glass
the lawn that receives her
like leaves of late autumn
leads down the slope
to the creek
within the ravine
where the thirst of the land's
made familiar
by lapping the clay

How Still, how still, how wonderfully still

the mud-bottom black
surface of Rondeau Bay
was almost always still
as the pooling
of much-used motor oil
bedizened by brilliant
prisms of gasoline rainbows
that threw
their perfumed circles
like multi-coloured quoits
of seven-hued sunlight dizzy with violet stirs
that painted the bay with small crafts smoking the far shores
and rather than wade
through the mucky shallows
of the sometimes weedy marl
clutching our candy-stripe terrycloth towels
we walked
the feet-burning length
of the tar-fragrant pier
to the dock ladders
where, as with a cooling of body fevers
we lowered ourselves
into the slow rise
of shining waters for we
were non-swimmers all
though we sank to the nose
like river hippos
denizens of the Congo and the Nile
we fancied ourselves to be Johnny Weissmuller
in dangerous deeps
meanwhile our drown-fearing mothers
clucking from the jetty
too far, too far come closer, don't splash,
it's time you came in, you'll cramp ...

all the quick children of the Busteed clan
still breathing the metallic rumour
mere floaters, children of the two-hour rule
infected by the lifelong aquaphobia
of dry land families, farm cousins, field hands
but we savored the after-scent of perilous liquids
the strange chemical odour of combustion
as we entered the dark indifference of dusk
that swallowed the tree-lines of home

The Day the Potawatomi Woman
Walked Away and into the Lake

today as I write
with the sun burning
on the bay
like the spirit fire of a water god
a daughter of the keepers of the flame
walked there
from her squatter's cabin
on the farm at home
and she stood alone
on the shore at land's end
with the deep blue invitation of the lake
calling her out and away
from the sand wash
where the cold stream
left its thirst at the end of the earth

bone woman
grown old
among thumb-grey fossils
and broken half shells
shining in pearlescent shades
of lost life

when I was a child
wading through combers
their white caps
breaking and foaming
where I breathed
with the slow seduction
cresting at my ribs
and sucking the pebbles
shoaling over my half-floating footfall

I might then
have had a thought for her
for the day she vanished
into sky fathoms
lifting her dark hair
like threads of light
too deep for the going
and she dropped like stone plunge
taking on the weight of darkness
perhaps recalling her people
from West Michigan, from Wisconsin
from Walpole, from all the disappeared
skunk sheds and outhouses
and junk holes and pear trees and
small dwellings
with time-crippled floors
and the cold fragrance
of an empty winter
staining black glass
while the unkempt bony-fingered lilac
clawed by weather
at the wind-and-rain weathered wood

and she's a ghost
of story
from long before
my long-dead uncle
was born to rumours
of her gone
when his father's father
set the barn stone
where it was sure to last
though it has not lasted
like ice refusing warm light
and the rain
like a thief in the seed

The Fox Remains

a solitary reynard crests the hill
at yards-end above the lake

a red startlement of flame
he burns along the green
rim of the cliff at the overlook

a drop-away of healthful fox smouldering
in the full vigor of wild-leafed autumn

he owns blue heaven
and is fearless in vanishing as is the spark
that follows the fuse elsewhere

all energetic crimson movement in the fur

no woman's mothy tippet
could wreck how he lives
a thriving fire lit within the kindle-bone
of his dry design

he masters the loping groom
on the close-cut grass

his calm heart quickening my own
as he disappears

I wave the scorched stick
charring the stone
of my most ancient and eternal soul

for the bent weed will soon enough winter
on the deepening of wind-scribed snow

so I write what melts away
but the fox remains
like a lamp left blazing in a dreamer's room

The Step Ladder

the step ladder
leans
like a three-legged creature
exhausted of purpose
one quarter crop lost in the wind
at the taking away of its
fraction of four

to the girls
who have set it there
it becomes
something of a work of art

a life-damaged sculpture
as though stolen from Jacob's stone-pillowed dream
with apples on branches
clinging to stems
keeping their faith in late autumn
junking cold heaven with fruit spoil
like the earbobs of angels
and bangles of witches

all time-tired weather
comes rattling sticks calling *winter, oh winter*
for climbing the absence
in an easing of darkness

where each ghost step is missing
the spirits are counting the air
in a splashing of shadow
while they're holding their breath
between worlds

Young Heroes of Terrace Beach

when we children walked
into the chill of the lake
where the waves crested
swelled then curled
and rolled backwards
with the slow inversion
of energy sucking the sand bed
and licking the perineum of our bodies
as though to excite
a strong desire for thrilled breathlessness as we
danced backwards on tiptoe
in a water ballet
stitched as we were
to the loom of sun-blue light
as the cross-current serpent
of a cold stream
shoaled downward from our knees
like sock fall
and we shivered inward
and were heart cooled
with goose-pimpled hair-prickled arms
raised like thin featherless wings
our toes en pointe
we were rocked on our pins
by the force
of a deepening push
as seven by seven
waves rose and shattered in soft swells
by the breakers
then sifting the stones
at the shoreline

and smoothing green glass
and shining half shells
to a pearlescent pink
reminiscent of something we dare not name
and the big-voiced water roared
like the universe waking the land
and if time took us in
to the ribs and in to the forelocks
we were lost to that joy
as our doomed flesh dipped to the heel

Cycling Home

I am cycling home
through the leaf scatter
of late summer
with tear-shaped scraps
of poplar loss
littering the street
like the soft amber lamentations
of the seven sisters
clinging to macadam
as though they were
the remnants of weeping
for what's lost in the not-quite coming on of autumn
and the gutters
at the curb
by the road shoulders
are deepening ecru
with the slow accumulation
of wind whisper
dry as old parchment
stemmed leaves veined
like the backs of a working man's hands

and I hear
the weather's sweet
largess
I hear bird song
the raw-voiced jay
complaining
as the beautiful will
and do
when they are lost
in the blue glory of a common sky

and there is also
the churring of crickets
the electric flang
of cicadas sawing the air
with metallic noise
and the close-by
stridulating of occupied grass
and I am awake to
the delicate whitewood asters
blushing at my ankles

and as I ride
I come upon a family of four
walking — an infant
asleep in a hooded buggy
that perambulator pushed
by a boy
followed by a man
a woman
each of the three
attentive to their palms
affixed with a *smart phone*
on which they are focused
as you would
were you nursing a sliver
from your lifeline

and it made me think
as I looked away in sadness
of how we are sometimes not here
even when the pain is most real

Afterword

... and furthermore ... *excerpts from an ongoing email correspondence between Don Gutteridge and John B. Lee (July 6, 2017 to February 19, 2018) with apologies for it being spontaneous and unedited, uncorrected expurgation taken directly from an extemporaneous electronic conversation:*

Hi Don

Your poem "Prayer," reminds me of a phrase I coined to describe how we remain in the memory of those who live on after us. I call it "the presence of absence" and I think I might have in this the quality of soul, the way a life remains in the mind of those who live on after an individual has passed away. This fond recall— the presence of absence is what I see in this poem. And those of us blessed to leave something of a record of our having been here, those of us given the gift of poetry and song, we are the keepers of the flame. The shamanism of the written word lights a fire in the wilderness to give comfort and meaning to those who come upon the sacred place of the still-living self.
All good things, John B.
(July 6, 2017)

Hi John

A wonderful poem. (The Luxury of Lust) How I envy the free-wheeling rhythms and collation of startling, perfectly apt images, the odd combination of open-endedness and focused precision. …but we all have our own voice. After all, poetry is a form of humans talking to one another, heightened by tropes and other majestic manoeuvers.

Best, Don

Hi Don

…I suppose as a farm kid it was never thought to shelter me from death. I've sat vigil with many loved ones on their deathbeds. It has always left me sad beyond words. I've been the one to take old dogs to the vets. I've felt the life force drain away and even as I write this I confess a sorrow beyond words.

We humans should not be sheltered from death and dying. I see in your elegy both the finality of your experience and the wisdom of acceptance.

All good things, John B.

(July 24, 2017)

Hi Don

As always a lovely poem. I read somewhere, or perhaps heard it said by someone, "all writing is ancestor worship," and although that may not be entirely true, if we live long lives we come to the point in our lives where time past exceeds the time yet to come and we are more memory than anticipation. And yet, if I am correct in my statement "we must imagine the past and remember the future." I am convinced that memory is an act of the informed imagination and we must acknowledge the ambiguity as it is with all imaginings … we are approximating the past, deepening the past with revivified experiences we come to understand the many faceted nature of all the threads of experience. The past has a grand simultaneity and we must tease apart the threads of experience to weave a story. The quality of truth that becomes available need not be slavishly adherent to the plod of facts. And the future that awaits us is endless with possibilities and we see into the past and look into the future. The past is a star long ago extinguished whose light we see, and the future seems a star unborn in a place not there.

Someone once said "time exists so that everything would not happen at once." In your poem the garden goes on without the woman it elegizes and without the mistress

of flowers. Like Gerard Manley Hopkins bittersweet poem on marigolds, the poem remains and blazes in sadness and loss and the reader breathes life into the paradox of existence, the comic tragic circumstances of the young girl and her existence in the moment and now she is gone forever …
All good things, John B.

Hi John
A near stream-of-consciousness poem. I admire and envy the free flow of images and linked ideas, one sliding into the next. I too wrote a poem before I went to sleep and am about to see if I recall it all. Poems forever surprise.
Don
(July 24, 2017)

Hi Don

…God bless all observances. The world is thick with meaning and we look and even sometimes see.
All good things, John B.
(August 2, 2017)

Hi John
Thanks. I guess I really never realized that I was making such a connection between widowhood and flower gardens. But my memory of her is always as a solitary figure in the garden, letting the flowers speak for her and blessing the neighbourhood in the bargain. She was telling us that despite her loss she was alive and thriving.
Best, Don
(August 2, 2017)

Hi John
The poems keep coming, especially those about my childhood days.

Hi Don
… Far too easy to mock the depth of field in a solitary memory let alone an entire childhood.
James Reaney talked about knowing everything in your world between your front door and the end of the sidewalk.
All good things, John B.

Hi John

It's amazing what triggers a poem for you. It seems to be the sudden confluence of events that sparks the need to resolve the issue on poetry.

Best, Don

Hi Don

I've always very moved when I read poetry written a thousand or more years ago. This morning I was reading a poem written sometime around 1101 by Su Shih and I quote the opening lines as an epigram here. The beauty of something preserved and thereby conserved in poetry for me involves the permanence of ephemera. The moment occurred in the poet's experience as related in the lovely language of dictionary music and I am reading it on this fine morning a thousand years after it was written.

The momentary and the eternal encompassed by the mind and body. As Bloom suggested of the metaphysics of our Christian saviour "Christ is a mortal god and we humans are immortal animals." This paradox, this ideal hinted at in the rhythms of the tides and the waves of the sea, and dare I say the ecstasy of human pleasures felt between lovers

… well, it boggles the mind that we might diminish our significance or exaggerate it for that matter.

This quotation introduces my poem "It is Moonlight Rocks this Boat — a love poem"
A gentle breeze rustles through the reeds and rushes —
I open the hatch to watch the rain, as moonlight floods the lake.

In a Boat, Getting Up at Night
Su Shih (1037-1101)
All good things, John B.

Hi John
You are the contemporary poet I most admire. Your emails have kept me writing and my ageing mind engaged.
Best, Don

Hi Don
You cannot imagine how honoured I am by your kind words and this tribute is much appreciated.
All good things, John B.

Hi John

You are right about writing as reading. As soon as I began writing seriously a year or so out of university, I had my first poem published in *The Fiddlehead* (six lines) but I immediately took out a subscription and began reading my contemporaries. I continued to read and subscribe to *Canadian Forum* and *West Coast Review* (all I can remember now). When some of my poems were accepted here and in the U.S. I thought I might actually be a poet (I always wanted to be a writer of some sort). I started buying and reading in 1962 or so books by Layton and Cohen and Purdy and Birney. And kept buying books until by 1980 I had over 500 in my collection. Last year I donated them to the Weldon Library, gratis. (My gift along with mss. To the university that supported me for a lifetime). By 1980 the poetry had dried up and I started to take novel writing seriously. Hence my reading focused on literary fiction (which I had also begun in the sixties) and my poetry reading tailed off. I didn't rediscover poetry (to my surprise) until almost 2000 and produced one slim volume. Then came the mysteries (I had read 500 mysteries over the years) and they kept me busy for four or five years. I produced three literary novels by 2000. The mysteries dried up on 2007 and to my delight I not only discovered poetry but developed a new

but time-worn style (short lyrics based on consonance, rhyme and assonance), and I just kept writing them (six volumes to date and three more on the hop). Sadly, I rarely read poetry these days (I find it too mentally stressful) except yours and that of a few friends, but I have read enough for one lifetime and that rooting in reading is what keeps producing verse.
Best, Don

Hi John
Delightful. The swing and sway of your rhythms is wonderful. I find the little contemporary poetry I read a-rhythmic. Imagine somewhere far back we were both entranced by Dylan Thomas, Tennyson, Gerard Manley Hopkins, Keats et al..
Best, Don

Hi Don
You are a major writer and your work has never stayed in a rut. I think back to the trilogy of documentary poems, *Riel, Tecumseh, and Coppermine*. I think of books like *God's Geography*, and *The Village Within*. And then I think of your recent books of po-

etry which are collections of small treasures on mortality and how we remember fondly and cherish the true sentiments of a mostly happy and often idyllic childhood all the while lamenting recent losses of old friends fixed as though in amber by memories of long ago and cherished in the present as good people preserved in the mind of those fortunate enough to survive the loss.

What I think great poets add to the human record involves sacralized humanity. Not the simple secular humanity of the zeitgeist of the here and now, but the eternal humanity of thousand-year-old and three-thousand-year-old and even six-thousand-year-old love. This morning I saw a piece in the paper about the first wine makers going back to almost five thousand B.C. I also think of the art in the caves of France, those ancestors going back to a time thirty to forty thousand years ago. We are keeping the flame alive, we who honour the human in poetry. The lyric and narrative impulse in great poetry makes you a major poet, at least that's the way I see it.

All good things, John B.

Hi John

Our correspondence and exchange of poems has kept my ageing mind and imagination alive these past years. Surely it must be a unique relationship among poets, one in mid form the other nearing the end of a long run. When I receive one of your beautiful poems I am immediately inspired to write one of my own. And this is the case with your poem about your mother's ashes. I recalled my first and rare visit to my mother's grave in the urn garden of Mount Pleasant Cemetery in London. I was taken aback when I saw her dates in bold relief and realized once again how young she was when she left us (54). Instead of revisiting that experience I prefer to remember her often and include her in my dreams and especially try to forget how she died. She complained of a sore neck and begged me to take her to the emergency. It was thirty below and I demurred. She insisted, so I took her and she caught pneumonia. When I went to pick her up for New Year's Day 1972 (which experience inspired Saving Grace: and Elegy) I found her dead on her couch.

Best, Don

Hi John

The death of five close friends over the past few years (and my age) have got me thinking about mortality, not in any morbid sense, but as a natural part of growing and the way the universe works.

Best, Don

Hi Don

I have found comfort and wisdom in poetry from a very young age, and from Thomas's "Refusal to Mourn the Death of a Child by Fire" "after the first death, there is no other." And Dylan Thomas was already gone from the earth by the time I began reading him. His "Do Not Go Gentle" that amazing villanelle on his father has always seemed ironic to me in that he encouraged his father to fight the darkness although he would eventually and essentially commit suicide by drinking himself into a coma.

The lacuna between the wisdom of deep need arising from inspired poetry, and the reality of being a human with foibles and shortcomings has always reminded me that we are seldom as wise as our poems. The truths that flow from the pen seldom come to play in the quotidian and often foolish actions.

These are the better angels of our nature, whispering onto the page, and then we glimpse the truth and move on.
All good things, John B.

Hi Don
Wow! "Ballast" is a beautiful poem. The line "until a song sings itself to your soul" would be a great title for a series of poems, and it seems you're writing a series.

The way the child awakens and life reveals itself in fascinating flickers of meaningful beauty reminds me of Bly's anthology *The Soul is Here for It's Own Joy*.
All good things, John B.

Hi Don

In a culture where fear and anger are stoked by the culture at large, where hatred and xenophobia are the subject of tweets by the bloviating narcissist in the White House, where entitlement and racism are systemic, where the twin toxins of wealth and fame infect popular culture, where the American Dream has been coopted by those who champion self-serving individualism even to the very highest ranks in public life, where sexism and racism are manifest in male entitlement and white lives are more highly valued, where warfare and militarism and law-and-order trample the rights of even the most law-abiding people of ethnic origin other than Caucasian, where right-wing fundamentalist Christian values trample people of other creeds, and where (as I heard on what is most likely the nadir of a 60 Minutes broadcast last evening) someone says out loud "I hate liberals …"

Sell an angry man a gun. Sell a frightened man a gun. Sell a man who hates, a gun. Sell an entitled and disturbed man a gun. And then drop him right in the middle of the most violent culture on the planet. This is the perfect recipe for chaos, mayhem and destruction.

America is fast becoming a bread and circuses empire of death. Arm the teachers. Arm the security guard. Arm the children. Arm the crossing guards. Arm the soccer moms. Arm the bus drivers. Arm the principals. Arm the lunch mothers. Pistols at dawn. Rifles at noon. Machine guns at the supper table. Derringers in the bedside table. No more bubble bath squirt guns for preschoolers. Pistols under the pillow.

Bazookas in the nursery. Now we feel safe?
Safety is a superstition.
All good things, John B.

Hi John
A beautifully written and passionate plea for civility amidst the anger and hate you describe so graphically. I am perpetually amazed at the power of your prose.
Best, Don

Don Gutteridge was born in Sarnia and raised in the nearby village of Point Edward. He taught High School English for seven years, later becoming a Professor in the Faculty of Education at Western University, where he is now Professor Emeritus. He has published seventy-one books: poetry, fiction and scholarly works in literary criticism and pedagogical theory and practice. He has published twenty-two novels, including the twelve-volume Marc Edwards mystery series, and thirty-eight books of poetry, one of which, *Coppermine*, was short-listed for the 1973 Governor-General's Award. In 1970 he won the UWO President's Medal for the best periodical poem of that year, "Death at Quebec." To listen to interviews with the author, go to: http://thereandthen.podbean.com. Don lives in London, Ontario.

John B. Lee was born and raised on a centennial farm near the village of Highgate in Kent County deep in the heart of Southwestern Ontario. Although he began his career as a teacher of English and Drama, he soon left the teaching profession to commit himself to life as a full-time writer. He has published nearly one hundred books, and is the editor of nearly a dozen anthologies. Appointed Poet Laureate of the city of Brantford in perpetuity, he is also Poet Laureate of Norfolk County for life, and Poet Laureate of the Canada Cuba Literary Alliance (2020-2022). Called 'the greatest living poet in English," by George Whipple, he is a recipient of well over one hundred prestigious national and international awards for his writing. He lives with his wife Cathy in a lake house overlooking Long Point Bay on Lake Erie in the town of Port Dover.

www.ingramcontent.com/pod-product-compliance
Lightning Source LLC
Chambersburg PA
CBHW020528080526
44583CB00013B/776